THE COMPLETE POTTER:
DECORATED EARTHENWARE

THE COMPLETE POTTER:
DECORATED EARTHENWARE

MIKE LEVY

SERIES EDITOR EMMANUEL COOPER

B. T. Batsford Ltd, London

British Library Cataloguing-in-Publication
Data.
A catalogue record for this book is available
from the British Library.

ISBN 0 7134 6770 3

Typeset by Servis Filmsetting Ltd
and printed in Hong Kong
for the publishers
B. T. Batsford Ltd
4 Fitzhardinge Street
London W1H OAH

Front cover
*One of a set of fruit bowls on
a theme exploring domestic interiors.
Thrown and slipped earthenware, 1989
(Mike Levy)*

Back cover
*Bowls, mugs and a plate decorated with Joe
Crouch's vibrant 'Mexico' pattern*

Frontispiece
*Thrown and slipped red earthenware bowl
with cobalt blues. Bowl by Mike Levy and
Christopher Gilvan Cartwright, paintings by
Christopher Gilvan Cartwright, 1990*

ACKNOWLEDGEMENTS

Photographs on pages 10, 11, 12, 16, 17, 19,
69 and 70 are reproduced by courtesy of the
Trustees of the British Museum; photographs
on pages 20, 23 and 38 are © Christie's; and
photographs on pages 13, 15, 23 and 30 are
by courtesy of the Board of Trustees of the
Victoria and Albert Museum.

Many thanks to all the potters who have
helped with information and photographs.
Photographs of the author making and
painting pots are by Catherine Boyce.
Thanks to Robert Maragh and Joe Crouch
for their much-needed help and patience.

CONTENTS

INTRODUCTION

As a means of self-expression, painting on pottery is wonderfully rewarding. When visitors to my workshop are invited to paint a pot, their excitement is effusive. They paint with initial unease on the white surface, but as the design progresses they become more and more excited.

When the finished pot comes out of the kiln and is presented to the painter, the look of amazement and pride is always worth any effort on my part. The glaze and firing have changed the pot into something permanent and independent from its painter, who has, by painting it, become a craftsperson. Every time they use the pot they will swell with pride and think 'I did that!'

Most people who do not make things regularly view the craftsperson with incredulity. They cannot understand how someone can actually make something as common as a bowl or a plate from scratch. The machine-made equivalents are so everyday, and their manufacture in factories so remote, that this creativity is outside the normal experience. The maker, however, knows that, once the appropriate skills and techniques are learned, it is the day-to-day creative application and the final results that are the reasons for making. Once the maker has acquired the necessary technical skills, it becomes possible to design and make with intuition and imagination.

Although the costs of the equipment and materials needed to set up a production workshop are relatively high, space-age technology has brought much equipment within many people's range. A new generation of small ceramic-fibre kilns, for example, can be plugged into a domestic socket and cost a few hundred pounds, making it possible for potters at home to own their own kilns, and for pottery to be made on the kitchen table (always bearing in mind the hazards associated with the materials). The student potter working in a class will also find the material and firing expenses fairly small for each item.

Potters who wish to make pots for the home have several advantages. The modest size of domestic objects such as mugs and bowls means that they can be decorated and fired quickly, and the results considered and applied to the next batch of pots. The fact that pots are everyday objects makes them approachable – there is not that daunting feeling, so common with canvas, that the painter has to produce a piece of art which is going to be framed and hung on the wall, and will therefore be seen and criticized by many people. Of course, a pot may end up on a plinth in a gallery, but the majority of its cousins will be happy on the table and the draining-board.

In this book I have restricted myself to explaining a small part of the process of producing a painted pot – the varied methods and techniques potters use to paint, glaze and finish pots – rather than dealing with the entire making processes. As the methods of clay preparation, throwing, handbuilding, press-moulding and slip-casting are all complicated subjects in themselves, I felt that an attempt to include them would limit the space that I have for discussing the main subject of the book: decoration. I have, therefore, assumed a knowledge of the basic making techniques. Any readers who need more information should refer to the other books in this series (see back cover) and to Further Reading on page 94.

Mike Levy, 1991

1 Skinny-dipping at Midnight, *thrown slipware vase by Mike Levy, 1991*

CHAPTER ONE

A SHORT HISTORY OF PAINTED POTS

A visit to the collections at the Victoria and Albert Museum or the British Museum in London, which have extensive ranges of pots on show, will illustrate the fact that painted pottery is anything but a new phenomenon. Indeed, this craft has been practised with extraordinary skill by potters from prehistoric times – almost since it was discovered that by baking clay you can preserve its shape and make it durable. The earliest pots were made at least eight thousands years ago, when the clay was formed into figures and small bowls by pinching and coiling it into shape.

A limited palette of browns and ochres was available from the differently coloured clays which occur in nature. Other colours were obtained using pigments made from vegetable matter and blood. Only the clays survived the temperature of the bonfire kiln, so the other colours would have been used to paint the pots after the firing. These same clays and pigments were used to paint the walls of the caves in which these people lived.

While the technology of pottery has developed to such an extent that it is now possible to make pots which have no evidence of being touched by the human hand, many cultures around the world are still making pots using methods very similar to those of prehistoric times (fig. 2). Indeed, there is much that contemporary pottery painters can learn about simplicity of design and directness of expression by looking at the wonderful patterns and designs on prehistoric pots in museums, as well as those produced by contemporary artisan potters around the world.

Pots have been painted with such a variety of styles and subjects that it is hard to attempt anything absolutely original. It is much better to look back at the traditions of earlier potters, learn from their best examples and adapt these lessons to new work.

My own work – designs produced by carving through a layer of light clay and coloured pigments to reveal a darker clay beneath – is similar in technique to that created by the Ancient Greek potters hundreds of years BC. Contemporary tin-glaze potters, who use techniques practised throughout contemporary Europe, are following a tradition of decoration started by the Islamic potters of the twelfth century or even earlier.

A comprehensive review of all the styles and subjects of historical pottery decoration would take many more pages than are available here, and I must content myself with some of the major examples. The subject is covered more comprehensively in *A History of World Pottery* by Emmanuel Cooper (Batsford, 1988).

2 Contemporary coiled dish from North Africa. Very similar in style and technique to the earliest pots found in Mesopotamia, dating from the fifth century BC. Painted with slips of tan and two browns

THE ORIGINS AND DEVELOPMENT OF PAINTED POTTERY

It is likely that the initial reason for painting pottery was a desire to produce more valuable spiritual and religious vessels. It may also be that pots were painted for much the same reason as they are today: people love to decorate their environment, and start by painting their everyday objects. A handmade pot – potentially a beautiful object in itself – has another dimension if it is also a painting.

As pottery developed around the world, different cultures would have had their own specific needs for both religious and everyday vessels. The reason for the emergence of the first painted pottery was probably devotional: the vessels were used for ritual and reverence, and surface decoration would have enhanced their importance. Early pots would have been quite a technical achievement, and would therefore have been valuable enough to use in ceremonies, along with other rare or precious materials. Before the development of metal and glass, pottery would have been the most sophisticated technology in use at the time.

Once making techniques such as fast-coiling, throwing and press-moulding had been developed, pots could be made *en masse* and would have become commonplace. Painting would have increased their value, as is still the case in places where pottery is made by hand for food use. Railway vendors in India serve tea in small thrown and fired cups which are used once and thrown away. Painted pottery, however, is kept for repeated use, along with vessels made of metal and glass.

The emergence of pottery is intrinsically linked to basket-making – in some cultures a more ancient craft than pottery – and fire. Water could be carried from its source to the camp by lining woven baskets with clay to make them watertight, and it would not have been long before hut fires led to the discovery that a burnt clay-lined basket left a hard shell. The earliest decorated pots were decorated with score marks to imitate the weave of the basket that the pot would replace, in much the same way that contemporary plastic planters are made to look like terracotta!

It is likely that the invention of pottery did not come about at a particular place, but developed independently in different pottery centres. The discovery of the first pottery-making techniques was inevitable in areas where clay was available, once the use of fire was commonplace. The potters of the Near and Middle East were the first to produce painted wares, the earliest-known being found in the Turkish Samarra region, from where the techniques spread.

As skills and techniques developed, the earlier bold, simple, geometric designs gave way to more complex images of animals, humans and landscape. While many of the centres of pottery production were permanent, there were also large movements of travelling people, who traded goods between different cultures over land and sea, bringing influences from other regions and having dramatic effects on the style and content of the pots they were trading. Pots were also used for packaging other goods, and the decoration would have been used as labelling, to distinguish one pot from another.

3 An example of the wonderfully exuberant designs of the Aegean potters of the second century BC, and characteristic of Minoan, Greek and Cypriot pottery. This jar is decorated with argonauts, and is one of the many marine-style pots made on the Greek mainland. Other pots had elaborate floral and abstract patterns. 1500 BC (British Museum)

THE ANCIENT MEDITERRANEAN

By 2000 BC the techniques had spread to the Mediterranean, and Cypriot, Cretan and Greek potters were producing wonderfully exuberant and wittily painted domestic wares, with images of marine life, bulls, birds and figures on chariots (fig. 3). By 1000 BC this type of pottery had developed into the well-known 'geometric' style of decoration used on forms such as amphora and krater, carried out on perfectly formed, thrown and turned vessels.

4   Two Greek hydria, with red-on-black and black-on-red designs. Thrown in buff clay and heavily turned to perfect the shape. A layer of a darker-red slip covers the buff clay

The jug on the left has figures of youths carrying water, painted with black pigment. The details are so fine that they must have been painted with a single-hair brush. Some details have sgraffito lines revealing the red clay. Athens, c. 1510 BC

The jug on the right shows two quarrelling heroes, and has black figures on a red background. The details are executed by carving through the slip layers to reveal the buff body. Other details are in darker red and white slips. Athens, c. 1510–1500 BC (British Museum)

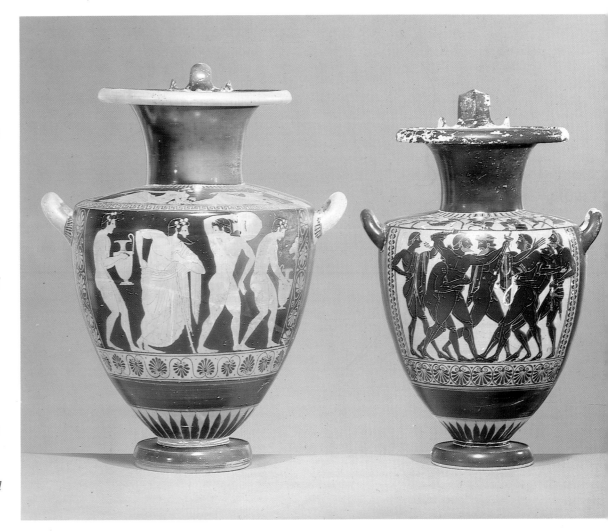

Research has shown that the Athenian potters developed an ingenious firing cycle of alternating oxidizing (oxygen-rich) and reducing (oxygen-starved) atmospheres in the kiln to produce the glossy black with which their designs were painted. Rather than paint

5   This Peruvian stirrup pot in the shape of a man dressed as an owl is typical of the wonderful sense of humour of many of these pots (British Museum)

the designs with an oxide-rich slip, they used a much finer version of the red slip, which, due to its finer particle size, vitrified at a lower temperature than the base slip. The reducing atmosphere in the kiln at high temperature had the effect of turning the red clay black, and the vitrified, painted slip details stayed black while the pot cooled in an oxygen-rich atmosphere which turned the body red again. This technique was developed before the Greeks had access to glazes, and gave a glossy surface rather than the matt-black associated with un-glazed oxide decoration.

Fig. 4 (previous page) shows two large water jugs (hydria). They are painted using the same techniques: one has black figures on red, and the other red figures on black.

Although the Romans had no tradition of *painted* pottery, they did develop fine skills in the manufacture of plain and incised pottery, and were responsible for the invention and spread of lead glaze from the Eastern Mediterranean to Europe and Asia.

With the growth of the Byzantine Empire, and subsequently the Islamic Empire, the techniques of painted pottery spread to Spain, and from there to northern Europe.

SOUTH AMERICA AND ASIA

The development of painted pottery was not confined to the continents of Africa and

6   A Mohican stirrup vase in the shape of a bird; the pot doubles as a whistle. 20cm (8in) high (British Museum)

Europe, but developed independently in Asia and the Americas, although there was no pottery made in Australia until the arrival of European settlers in the eighteenth century.

Before the European invasion of South America, pottery was the major method of manufacturing everyday objects used for cooking, storage, music and architecture, all made without the use of the wheel. Many of these objects were painted with exuberant designs, using slips. Mineral and vegetable pigments were painted on after firing to produce colourful designs. The famous Peruvian, pre-Colombian stirrup vessels (figs. 5 & 6) were handbuilt, painted and burnished, with abstract and figurative images.

The Chinese are famous for producing the earliest porcelain, but they also used lead glazes on earthenware pots during the T'ang dynasty of the seventh and eighth centuries (fig. 7). These coloured glazes were probably imported from the West, and were typically stained with iron oxide (brown) and copper oxide (green). When the Chinese developed high-fired and decorated porcelain in about AD 900, trade routes carried it to Persia, where the whiteness and fine quality surpassed the copper-blue glazed earthenware being produced there.

7 A T'ang dynasty lidded jar. White earthenware, decorated with ochre and green glazes. 8cm (3¼in) high (Victoria & Albert Museum)

8 This large, handbuilt sprigged vase by Kate Malone is similar in technique to the T'ang dynasty jar on the previous page. 20cm (8in) high, 1990

Experiments to reproduce this white pottery using earthenware clays led to the discovery that the addition of tin oxide to the glaze made it white and opaque. These pots were often decorated with metallic lustres, and with oxides which were painted on the glazed surface and sank into the glaze during the firing to produce wonderfully rich colours. This technique spread to Europe and across North Africa to Spain in the twelfth century.

TIN GLAZING

By the fifteenth century, tin glazing had spread from Spain to Italy, via Majorca, where it acquired the name *majolica*. In Italy the process reached wonderful heights. The Renaissance inspired a great tradition of heavily painted, thrown platters and jars with wonderfully exuberant designs of mythology and religion, portraits, animals and patterns of fruit and flowers (fig. 10, overleaf).

9   A beautiful Isnik (Persian) dish-imitation of Chinese porcelain. Tin-glaze with blue-and-black painting (Victoria & Albert Museum)

10 Superb example of Italian Renaissance majolica. This large dish, from the pottery town of Deruta in Umbria, has a portrait of a woman with an inscription. Thrown in buff earthenware with white tin-opacified lead glaze. C. 1500 (British Museum)

As trade links grew, Chinese porcelain reached Europe, and tin-glazed pottery began to be produced in Chinese styles, for the same reasons that the earlier Islamic potters had developed tin glazing: to imitate porcelain. Some of the most striking blue-and-white tin-glazed pottery was produced at Delft in Holland from the mid-seventeenth century (fig. 11), though chinoiserie was also produced extensively in Britain.

The techniques of slip decoration, especially sgraffito, were developed by the potters of the Byzantine Empire in the eleventh century, often in conjunction with coloured lead glazes. These pots, and their making techniques, found their way via trade routes to Central Europe and were instrumental in bringing about a revival in painted-pottery production.

11 *Blue-and-white Delft chinoiserie dish. The original Chinese figures have been replaced by people with Dutch costumes. Tin-glazed earthenware, c. 1650–1700 (British Museum)*

12   A pair of tin-glazed jars by Daphne Carnegy, 1986

After the departure of the Romans from northern Europe, pottery production went into decline. In England it reverted to the technical qualities of the Iron Age, with rough, handmade pots being low-fired in bonfire kilns. Roman techniques of wheel-throwing and glazing were gradually re-introduced from Europe, where they had survived, and by the thirteenth century slip-decorating was commonplace. This tradition continued to develop until it reached its peak in the seventeenth and eighteenth centuries. The most famous of the potters whose work has survived from this period were Thomas Toft and the Simpson brothers, who made large dishes with Royal portraits, and designs with mermaids and animals (see fig. 13 and fig. 71 on page 69).

13   This seventeenth-century platter was produced by Ralph Simpson, one of the leaders of the tradition of English slipware. Red earthenware with a yellow glaze over white and light and dark brown slips. 42cm (16¾in) diameter, Burselm, c. 1700 (British Museum)

As the industrial age developed, European pottery became more and more technically sophisticated. Ornate moulding and elaborate printing techniques were invented, which removed the visibly 'handmade' quality from pottery. Intricately detailed porcelains were produced in France and Britain, with equally elaborate painting and applied decoration. While these mechanically produced pots were often of exceptional quality, they lacked the wonderfully expressive nature of their handmade cousins.

CRAFT BECOMES FINE ART

Once the industrial age had liberated production from the artisan's workshop, many traditional skills started to disappear as their products were replaced by machine-made alternatives. Alarmed by the soulless nature of mass production, the Arts and Crafts Movement, which arose in the second half of the nineteenth century, saw the use of craft processes and natural materials as a more attractive way of producing useful objects.

14 A beautiful press-moulded earthenware platter with a slip-trailed bird. Made by Elijah Comfort and decorated by Michael Cardew. The design was trailed with white slip on the leatherhard clay. A clear glaze covers the dish, and the slip lines have a copper-green glaze painted over them. c. 1932 (photograph courtesy of Christie's)

The pottery on show at Crystal Palace in the Great Exhibition of 1851 was wonderfully elaborate and technically superb, but seemed to derive its appeal from these qualities, rather than any superior style of form or decoration. This deficiency led to the setting up of art schools which would train students to work with industry to produce improved design and decoration. There was still, however, a separation between design of form and application of decoration.

The leading exponent of the Arts and Crafts Movement was William Morris, who, along with his contemporaries Edward Burne-Jones and Dante Gabriel Rossetti, inspired artists to design objects from scratch, looking at both form and decoration. This led to artists working with industry, and, ultimately, to artists working in workshops to produce objects themselves. A leading potter in this group was William De Morgan, whose pottery studio (established in 1872) produced pottery and tiles which had elaborate decoration on simple shapes and featured dragons, foliage, fish and boats. They were painted in rich 'Persian-style' underglaze and metallic lustre (fig. 15).

15 White earthenware plate by William De Morgan, decorated with coloured slips, c. 1890. De Morgan also worked extensively with lustres (British Museum)

THE OMEGA WORKSHOP

One particularly interesting group of artist-designers was based at the Omega Workshop, which was established in 1913 in Bloomsbury, London. Unlike the Arts and Crafts Movement, it employed artists to carry out designs on shapes made by others.

Their main premise was that their products, including pots, were a commercial concern, and that artistic skills could be applied to decorative art objects as well as to canvas. They were particularly interested in colour and the decorative qualities of painted designs, and members of Omega would design and decorate in a variety of materials. The lively colours and confident brushstrokes covered virtually everything in sight.

While the pots were often freely thrown and heavy, many of them had a vibrant 'living' quality, with no hint of caution in the application of design and colour. In addition to pots, they painted fabrics and designed furniture and screens, all of which have had considerable influence on design in the latter half of this century.

The ideas of the Omega Workshop directly contradicted the philosophy of the potter Bernard Leach, who set up his pottery at St Ives, Cornwall in 1920. Having been trained in Japan, he believed that the perseverance and practice of a craft tradition could bring about spiritual and social enlightenment. This was also a confirmation of the ideas and theories of William Morris, who advocated that everyday objects could be handmade at reasonable prices.

ARTISTS AND DESIGNERS

At the same time that Leach and the Omega Workshop were working in Britain, a different approach was being taken on the Continent, where artists worked with artisan potters. In France, the painter Dufy was working with the potter Artigas to produce wonderful pots and tile pieces (Artigas was later to work with both Picasso and Miró). As these painters were decorating ready-made pots, there was the opportunity for immediate self-expression, and pots were available to paint at any stage of the making process. Although the lack of technical skills meant that there was little scope for correcting any mistakes during painting, the fact that someone else was the maker gave them artistic freedom.

In the 1940s Artigas worked with a fellow Catalan, Joan Miró. Whereas Dufy was primarily a 'decorator' of pots, Miró had much more of a 'hands-on' approach, extending his experiments to include sculpture, mosaic and massive tile pieces. Miró's painting technique was applied to pottery in a highly successful, immediate way, particularly in his use of oxides and coloured glazes. Here, there was no notion of the pottery vessel as a domestic object – it became a piece of art, as did everything Miró touched.

At the same time, and in a similar way, Pablo Picasso was working in clay at the workshop of Suzanne and Georges Ramie, at Vallauris in the South of France. Like Miró, Picasso had a 'hands-on' approach and an immediate affinity for clay, working quickly and with great enthusiasm to produce some of the finest examples of expressive pottery decoration ever made.

16 (Right) This beautiful Omega vase was made by Phyllis Keyes and painted by Duncan Grant in 1937. White earthenware with underglaze painting (Victoria & Albert Museum)

17 (Far right) Decore Feuilles, painted by Pablo Picasso with coloured slips on a 'green' (unfired) pot. Painted areas are glazed over the decoration. Conceived and made as an artwork, rather than a useful vessel, much of the surface is left unglazed. Stamped and dated underneath 'Madoura Plein Feu 2.50'. 58cm (23in) high, February 1950 (photograph courtesy of Christie's)

The series of press-moulded dishes on page 38 illustrates how effective drawing through layers of pigment and glazes can be. These designs are made up of a few simple strokes, and areas of colour are produced by a combination of slips, oxides and glazes. These were used together without too much concern for their technical viability, but rather as an experiment to see what would happen in the kiln. The materials used to make the original images on the raw unfired pots bore very little resemblance to the colours and surface quality when the pots came out of the kiln. Picasso would have had a row of dishes with creamy-looking liquids in various shades of greys and browns, and would only have had test pieces for reference.

Collaboration between industry and designer-painters in the 1920s and 1930s led to the much-acclaimed pottery of Clarice Cliff (right) and Susie Cooper. Trained as china painters in industry, they both went on to design and produce innovative new shapes and popular handpainted designs for cheerful, elegant tableware. The illustrator Eric Ravillious is also notable for his work with Wedgwood in the 1940s and 1950s.

MODERN CRAFT

In recent years, decorated pottery has enjoyed a renaissance, with makers crossing the traditional boundaries of art and craft. The contemporary 'designer-maker' practises the skills of the pre-Industrial Revolution artisan in a way of which William Morris would have been proud, although with the profusion of well-designed, affordable industrial pottery on the market, handmade pots are now at the luxury end of the scale.

There is also a group of makers who are working in an intermediate discipline by taking the products of industry and 'customizing' them – china painters, for example. In addition, many makers have found that part of the making process can be carried out in a factory, thus cutting their

18 *This bowl was designed by Clarice Cliff as part of her 'Bizarre' range. This particular pattern is called 'Fantasque'. Made at Wilkinson Ltd, early 1930s*

overheads and production time. There is an increasing need for a full-time maker to have a range of repeatable stock with a wholesale price list, alongside their 'one-off' work. A handbuilder or thrower will therefore have a model of a pot reproduced by a slip-casting factory, and can then paint and glaze the pots in batches without having to make each one individually.

The shelves of kitchen shops, galleries and department stores are increasingly full of brightly painted tableware, while the production stoneware common in the 1970s and 1980s is becoming relatively scarce. This may be because the palette has been greatly extended by the availability of a wider range of colours, enabling the studio potter to make pots with 'user-friendly', brightly coloured underglazes and glazes.

Another reason could be that the renewed emphasis on ceramics as a method of artistic expression differs philosophically from Bernard Leach's orientally-inspired search for spiritual enlightenment, which influenced many potters of the 1970s. This is partly because, for the last twenty years, art schools have taught *ceramics* alongside painting, sculpture, illustration and design, with studio pottery being seen as a craft discipline rather than a means of artistic expression. Moreover, many of the more famous potters since the 1950s have been painters and sculptors who work with clay, such as Lucie Rie, Hans Coper, Gordon Baldwin, Carol McNicoll and David Garland.

CHAPTER TWO

INSPIRATION FOR DESIGN

Potters have traditionally drawn on a wide range of subjects for their designs. The earliest designs were abstract lines and squiggles – obvious extensions of the making process – which could be applied to the pot as it revolved on the wheel, or during the glazing process. Many pot shapes suggest different geometric designs which 'fit'. Often a pot is noticeable for the fact that its design does *not* fit, making it unusual and sometimes very successful. I sometimes play with this idea when developing a design, by painting a border round a bowl and then making an element of the main design come over the edge into the border.

Figurative designs often use fruit, flowers, animals and human figures. Birds and fish are particularly popular, and are used in most cultures. Portraits of patrons were popular in Renaissance Italy, and kings and queens were favourite subject matter in seventeenth-century England. Religious and mythological images and pastoral scenes have also been widely used. Among the most engaging pots

of all are those which depict scenes of everyday life, and I use this theme extensively in my work (fig. 19).

When looking at pots in museums and books for inspiration, it is important to use favourite elements rather than to try to copy the whole style. Look at how one potter has painted a face, for example, or how a style depicts foliage. Your scope can extend much further than just pottery: manuscript illustration, embroidery, stained glass and other applied arts have traditions of strong design and sensitive detail.

19 One of a set of fruit bowls on a theme exploring domestic interiors. Thrown and slipped earthenware, 1989 (Mike Levy)

20 *Sandy Brown is a potter whose expressive use of coloured slips, engobes and glazes produces bright and lively tableware*

Other sources of inspiration can include folk arts and crafts such as Aboriginal painting, Mexican papier mâché, and South American textiles. The scope is endless: open eyes and a receptive brain can soak up designs and process them into something new and exciting.

DEVELOPING A DESIGN

Once you have decided on the subject matter for your design, the next stage is to develop it in such a way that it 'fits' the pot. This can be achieved in two ways. Firstly, the image should belong on the pot: subject matter and form should 'work' together, a purely subjective decision which experience will teach.

Secondly, scale is important: the size of the shapes which make up the design should be in keeping with the dimensions of the pot. One way of doing this is to draw a design in a round outline and then carefully transfer it in one piece on to a dish, so that it sits in the centre with a border all round the edge. I prefer to arrive at a design which I think is suitable, and to draw it on the pot so that the shapes within the design relate to the shape of the pot, but are not necessarily contained by its boundaries. When drawing a figure on a fruit bowl, for example, I will place the oval of the head in a position and size that I feel looks right, in the knowledge that the whole figure will never fit on that side of the bowl. This keeps the image one step ahead of my

pencil, and the subsequent need to continue working the design out as I draw it on the pot keeps it fresh and fluid. The usual solution is to take the figure over the edge of the bowl and around on to the outside, ignoring the barriers of the rim and foot.

The fluidity of the scribbled design is difficult to maintain, especially if there are several processes involved in the painting. I often find that a quickly drawn design which has a quality of looseness and movement stiffens up when it has been finished with a sgraffito line. A remedy is to work quickly with as little worked-out detail as possible. In other words, think on your feet! Potters who can work with paints in a spontaneous and fluid way are few and far between, as it is a difficult knack to apply the paint unselfconsciously. Sandy Brown (fig. 20) achieves this very successfully, working with stoneware clay in a very 'earthenware' way, exploiting the qualities of the new high-temperature colours.

In the following chapters I will explain how to arrive at a design and apply it to the surface of a pot with colourful, painterly results. It is important, however, that these guidelines are not taken as hard-and-fast rules. All makers adapt and combine materials and techniques to develop a way of working which suits their own personal style. Pottery is art and science combined and it is the individual maker who develops the most suitable methods to express his or her own ideas. Feel free to combine these techniques

and develop your own – you will discover your own unique way of working.

Before any attempt is made to paint a pot, careful thought must go into developing the design. It is rare for a painter to attack a canvas without first making preliminary studies and sketches. Decisions have to be made about subject matter, format and scale. The shape and size of the pot to be painted will have some bearing on the design: the restrictions imposed by a fruit bowl's related inside and outside surfaces are very different from the continuous curves of the outside of a round vase, for example. Moreover, a steep-sided bowl will suggest a relationship between the paintings inside and out, which will relate to each other depending on the angle of view. The drawings overleaf show how different forms demand different decorative solutions.

In much the same way as a pot is divided up into elements (often named after body parts, i.e., neck, belly, foot, lip) a design can take different sections of the pot into consideration. A border design may be used to formalize a design on a platter in much the same way as a frame will 'finish' a painting. The same border can be painted round the neck of a jug and down the handle, emphasizing the design or matching it to other pots with different paintings. In this way I relate all the pots in my tableware range with two contrasting border designs (a repeated scroll and black and white 'piping') so that a variety of pots will match.

1.

2.

3.

Tall shapes have designs which work around the pot (1,2) or divide the surface (3)

Plates, bowls and dishes can have separate, or related images inside and out or top and bottom.

Surface decoration can be divided into two categories: *image* and *pattern*. If a design is made up of a picture, depicting, for example, figures, a landscape or a bowl of fruit, it is an *image*. A *pattern* is made up of repeated images arranged in such a way that they cover the surface of the pot, and can also consist of an arrangement of different images. In order to arrive at a pattern, you must develop the initial images. To illustrate this, I will explain the workings which led to the fish pattern which is one of my standard tableware designs (see page 33).

CREATING A PATTERN

STAGE ONE: RESEARCH

If a pattern is to be successful, care must be taken to develop the initial images of which it will consist. Traditional images are often used – flowers, fruit, animals, fish, birds,

21 *Different shapes demand different treatments when it comes to planning the decoration. Tall vases and jugs need a design which moves round the pot. More open shapes such as bowls and dishes can have inner and outer designs which relate to each other*

astrological signs, suns and moons – and sources for these images are all around us. My favourite places to look are books of images for graphic designers, old woodcut sample books and fabric design. Museums of decorative art and design such as the Victoria and Albert Museum in London are treasure houses, full of artefacts with wonderful images. Your images may be inspired by paintings in galleries or by books; many of my earlier figurative pots were painted with figures taken from an old and well-thumbed book of Raphael drawings.

There is of course no reason why your pattern should be made up of traditional images: you could use electronic calculators and portable phones. I once painted a fruit bowl for a desk, which had all the objects on the desk making up the pattern, including pens, paper clips, typewriter and anglepoise light!

STAGE TWO: DEVELOPMENT

Once you have arrived at the initial image, it must be developed so that it can be incorporated into a pattern which can be applied on both flat and curved surfaces. It is well to take into consideration the techniques which will be used for the final painting. My decoration techniques rely heavily on the sgraffito line made by incising through a white slip to reveal red clay, and this line is therefore an important element in the design. Other techniques can involve flat areas of colour or line brushwork.

The initial idea for my fish pattern came from a Chinese vase with a blue-and-white traditional carp design in the Victoria and Albert Museum (fig. 22, overleaf). By carefully copying the design in my sketchbook, I was able to take home an image which could then be adapted and altered to my own style. Re-drawing the image over and over, using tracing paper or thin copier paper, 'streamlined' and altered it to take on my own style. As my fish developed, it gained an extra eye and variations of body markings. The lips also acquired a variety of expressions. I eventually developed a range of fish images with different positions, markings and expressions, which could fit together into a pattern.

STAGE THREE: ARRANGING IMAGES INTO A PATTERN

By copying or photocopying the images a number of times and cutting these out, you can arrange them on a big sheet of paper in different ways until a satisfactory pattern emerges. The enlarging and reducing button on a photocopier can come in very handy here, as this is the stage to start thinking about the scale of the images on the finished pot. Some of the fruit-bowl designs in my fish-pattern range have one large fish, while others have many smaller ones (see fig. 27 on page 33). Once you have arrived at a successful arrangement of images, stick them down and trace or copy them on to another sheet of paper.

22 *(Left) This blue-and-white porcelain vase in the Victoria & Albert Museum inspired my fish pattern (Victoria & Albert Museum)*

23 *A detail of fig. 22*

24 *Line drawing of fish design*

25   *The pattern is worked out by repeatedly drawing, copying and arranging the elements until a coherent design has developed*

STAGE FOUR: BACKGROUND

In order for the pattern to have a cohesive structure, it must be tied together by a background pattern which can fill the gaps between the images. This is very important in pottery decoration, as it is unusual for a pattern to fit on to a curved surface without awkward gaps. A background pattern can fill these gaps without looking contrived.

After trying out various marks, squiggles and swirls I arrived at a background pattern based on joined-up spirals, executed in two-colour wax resist and resembling a watery batik (see fig. 54 on page 57). My other patterns use different marks. The sun pattern (see pages 60 and 62) has stars on a dark blue background; a floral pattern has simple squiggles which can be adapted to fit the size and shape of the gap. Solid colour and brushmarks can also serve this purpose.

STAGE FIVE: COLOUR

By copying the design several times, you can decide on the colourways of your pattern in much the same way as a fabric designer will develop a swatch of related materials. Obviously it will be a waste of time using colours and marks which are not available with the materials you have, so bear in mind what is at your disposal. Mix paints and inks to the colours and opacity of the fired

26 *Line drawing of border designs*

ceramic materials you will be using, or find suitable felt-tip pens and crayons.

Very different results can be achieved by altering the tonal balance of the design – try dark and light backgrounds. Colours juxtaposed or used one on top of the other can give wonderful results: I find the most successful patterns contrast light and dark colours and hues. In this case bright yellow, orange, lime green and pink fish swim on a dark blue swirl background. The pattern is further enhanced by giving the fish colourful stripes and spots.

STAGE SIX: BORDERS

After working out several colour variations and deciding which are the most successful, the final stage before applying the design to the pot is deciding whether to have a border design, and, if so, what this design will be. You may decide that your pattern looks better without a border, though it can be fun to make the pattern interact with and overlap the border in places. The shape of the pot to be painted will also have an influence.

Borders can be designed in much the same way as patterns – they are basically a repeated image or mark (fig. 26). Reference to architectural friezes or wallpaper patterns, book-illustration borders or picture frames can be stimulating.

27 A large fruit bowl with the fish pattern. The sequence of painting for this design is shown on pages 54–60

ONE-OFF DESIGNS

If the pot is going to have a one-off, all-over image, rather than a pattern, care must be taken to develop a design which will sit successfully on the curved surface and fit the shape. After years of practice this is now almost automatic, and my preparation usually involves scribbling the design on the workbench and then straight on to the pot.

However you develop your image, it is important to keep some vitality in the marks, or the fired pot will look lifeless. Be prepared to adapt the design at the last minute, rather than slavishly tracing or copying it. Don't be afraid of the pot, but attack it with the decoration. It only becomes precious when it is glazed and fired, and if it goes wrong you can always make another.

SOURCE MATERIAL

In much the same way that a pattern is developed, care must be taken to decide on an appropriate subject for the image. Traditional subjects such as still lifes and landscapes can be enlivened with contemporary objects; figures can be wearing modern clothes. Many of my pots are covered with astronomical signs such as suns and moons – tarot and playing cards are also good source material – and I have adapted the sun and moon designs and given them bodies. Pictures of Hindu gods which I collected in India also provide inspiration, with their amazing use of vibrant colour.

STAGE ONE: WORKING OUT THE DESIGN

Unless your pot is a flat, rectangular platter, you will have to adapt the design to fit on to the curved, continuous surface. This can be an advantage, as it enables you to tell a story as the eye moves around the pot. You must bear in mind that the left and right sides of the flat image will join on a round pot, and you should be careful to arrange the image in such a way that this point is not seen as the back of the pot. A round vase or bowl should work equally well from any angle.

This is also where elements of pattern design can be used. There will be gaps on the pot, where other decoration can be inserted to provide interest, so that the design is

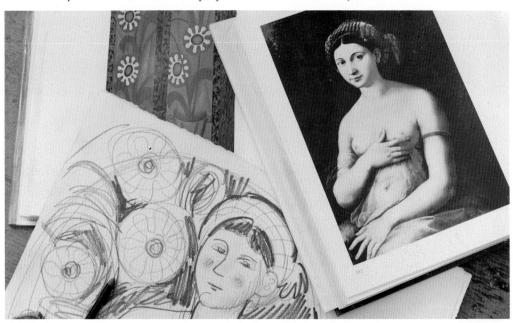

28 By gathering a diverse collection of inspiration and reference material, it is possible to draw elements from different places to create new and unique designs. This drawing was developed using a Raphael painting and an Omega screen design

accessible from any angle. This will become clearer as I describe how the design is worked out and applied.

STAGE TWO: ARRANGING THE DESIGN

Once you have your image, you must arrange it to fit the pot. The original image is drawn, or the source is copied, on to a large sheet of paper so that it is removed from the constraints of its original border (whether this is an actual border, surrounding images, or the edges of the page).

Copies of this image are then made by tracing or photocopying, and are stuck next to or overlapping the first image. (This is also a good way to develop border designs.) Other elements or images can then be designed to fit into the gaps to make a homogeneous design, always bearing in mind the shape of the pot. If the image is of, say, a mermaid, then fish, shells, a harp, an octopus or a sailor's cap could be used to fill in a gap. If this extra image has humour in it, this will draw attention and tie the design together well.

STAGE THREE: COLOUR

Copy the finished line image a number of times and experiment with the colours you will be using to develop the final design. Different colourways can completely transform the feeling of a design – consult fabric samples for inspiration.

29 *The finished design*

CHAPTER THREE

MATERIALS AND PAINTING TECHNIQUES

Before discussing the many ways in which pottery materials can be used to make decorated pots, and the various techniques, it is important to understand the nature of the materials themselves.

CLAY

Clay is a naturally occurring material which is the result of rock erosion over millions of years. It has a variety of appearances, ranging from a deep reddish-brown to a creamy-white. The darker the colour, the more iron oxide and other vegetable impurities there are present. White clays therefore have very few impurities. Clays can also contain (or have added) other materials such as sand or ground-fired clay (grog), which alter its texture, and also its resistance to heat shocks.

Earthenware, stoneware and porcelain offer potters a wide variety of clay bodies from which to choose. They can be mixed to suit a particular purpose.

EARTHENWARE CLAYS

Earthenware clays can be fired to temperatures as high as 1200°C (2192°F), although most mature at lower temperatures (around 1000°C [1832°F]). Some potters who wish to paint their pots favour lower-temperature earthenware clays because there is a wider range of colouring oxides available, many of which burn away at higher temperatures. Prepared industrially produced underglaze colours and body and glaze stains further extend the colour range, providing an extensive palette for earthenware potters.

Earthenware clays range from a creamy-white to a deep red, with browns and ochres in between. Red clays have an iron-oxide content of 6–8%, which has the effect of lowering the maturing temperature. Many white earthenware clays can actually be fired to stoneware temperatures with the addition of some grog to give extra strength.

STONEWARE CLAYS

Some stoneware clays occur naturally, and can be mixed by adding other materials to earthenware clays to raise the maturing temperature. When fired, stoneware clay has a dense, solid quality, with none of the fragile feel of earthenware. The high maturing temperature of stoneware (1200–1300°C [2192–2372°F]) means that only highly temperature-stable oxides such as iron, manganese, cobalt and chrome can be used for painting.

PORCELAIN CLAY

Porcelain is a pure-white clay prepared from China clay, ball clay and feldspar or Cornish (Carolina) stone, and matures at around 1260–1300°C (2300–2372°F). If potted thinly it can be translucent when fired to vitrification.

GROG

If you need to make your clay body more open – to give it strength or texture, or to raise the firing temperature – you can add grog. This is a clay which has been fired and then ground to a powder. Adding it to the clay enables you to throw larger pots without risk of collapse, or to handbuild more quickly. Molochite is a white version of grog, made from fired and powdered China clay.

GLAZES

Earthenware glazes are a distinct, glossy 'skin', a thin layer of glass which has been melted on the surface of the pot, unlike stoneware glazes which combine with the pot. Some of the earliest earthenware glazes consisted of lead oxide (galena), which was sprinkled on the surface and fluxed the clay during firing. It was discovered that by adding metal oxides, different colours could be produced.

Raw-lead oxide is no longer used in the pottery studio for health and safety reasons, though glazes with lead compounds can be made up by using lead frits – compounds which have been fired and powdered to produce non-soluble materials that are safe to handle. (All powdered materials should be handled with extreme care in the workshop, as they are all potentially hazardous.)

Glazes can also be based on alkaline frits, which, when used with copper oxide, give the characteristic turquoise colours associated with Ancient-Egyptian pottery. The chemical make-up of the glaze has a large bearing on the colours produced when fired.

A wide range of ready-to-use glazes is available in powder form from craft and pottery suppliers. It is often cheaper in the long run, however, to make your own, even though this means investing in all the ingredients first.

SLIPS AND ENGOBES

A basic slip is a liquid clay, sieved to make it smooth and homogeneous. Other materials can be added to colour the slip, to give it texture or to improve the 'fit' on the clay body.

Engobes are slips which vitrify to a smooth, typically satin surface, and in content fall somewhere between slips and glazes.

COLOURING MATERIALS

By adding small amounts of other materials to your clay, slip or glaze, you can alter its colour and/or opacity. Tin oxide or zirconium silicate, for example, can be added to a clear earthenware glaze to produce a white, opaque glaze, suitable for in-glaze painting (see page 70). The addition of 10% is a usual amount. Metal oxides and carbonates can be added in small quantities to colour slips and glazes. For further details and recipes, see pages 91–3.

Additional colours can be obtained by using industrially produced underglaze colours and glaze and body stains. These contain complex mixtures and are highly refined to give a wider range of colours. This makes them expensive, with colours such as red and orange – obtained from rare-metal oxides – costing much more than the others.

Stains should be added to bodies, slips and engobes at 5–15%, and to glazes at 4–10%. Some colours will need to be sieved through a 200s-mesh screen to remove any speckles.

Enamels are low-temperature coloured glazes which have been fritted (fired and ground to a powder) to enable them to be applied to an already glazed surface before being re-fired.

PAINTING WITH PIGMENTS

Stunning results can be obtained by simply painting colours on to the surface of the pot with a brush. The nature of ceramic materials provides a wealth of qualities, obtainable by adding various different materials to the 'paints'. Here trial and error, and experience, will produce the desired effects.

At its most simple, a picture can be painted on a white-clay pot – raw or biscuit-fired – using a pigment in suspension in water. Oxides of iron, cobalt, manganese and chrome can be used to give browns, blues and greens, and a fairly extensive palette can be built up by mixing these oxides together. The glaze which will cover the design will also have an effect on the finished colour and quality of the brushmarks. Experimenting with combinations of these materials can give exciting results.

30 *A group of Picasso plates from 1956/7. These plates demonstrate the range of techniques at the disposal of the pottery painter, and emphasize the way that the use of materials can influence the feel of the finished piece (photograph courtesy of Christie's)*

(Top left) A white glaze was used to paint the design thickly on to the dish. After firing, the clay body was stained black, the glaze remaining white; (Second left) A bullfight design on the plate was simply painted in a black oxide mixture. The marks on the border were made with a sharp tool in the leatherhard clay; (Bottom left) This floral design was trailed with a slip rich in copper, to give a metallic effect; (Top right) The hands and fish were modelled into the dish's surface, and details were painted with oxides. A clear glaze was applied over some areas, leaving others unglazed; (Second right) The design was applied with white slip, and clear and coloured glazes were applied. The coloured glaze has settled into the dips, emphasizing the design; (Bottom right) The horse was painted in black and covered with wax, which was also used to define the rim. The grey background slip was then applied. After biscuit firing the clear, red and blue glazes were added

As oxides are finely ground and soluble in glaze, they will disperse evenly. Stains and underglaze colours, however, may need further grinding to enhance their effect. A glaze or slip coloured with a stain will therefore need stirring to make its colour even. Glazes containing strong colouring oxides may need sieving to avoid speckles.

The availability of industrially produced ceramic colours considerably increases the palette at the potter's disposal. Even colours which are notoriously difficult to achieve with oxides are now available, such as bright reds, yellows and oranges. These are made possible by refined industrial techniques and the use of rare-metal oxides, and are virtually impossible to prepare in the workshop.

Whether you buy your colours or make your own, they can be painted on raw or biscuit pottery using a suitable medium. Various materials can be used – I have tried sugar-based media such as golden syrup and honey, egg yolks, oils and glycerine. Pottery suppliers sell bottles of medium, which work but do not seem any more suitable than those mentioned above.

I have found through trial and error that a 50/50 mixture of glycerine and cream-consistency white slip produces a medium which I can mix into a thick paste with the underglaze colour. This can be diluted with water on the brush if necessary. This gives me a paint which will cover the pot thickly, with no flaking or smudging, to give a good, strong result.

Some of the media mentioned here will resist a glaze, and so they will need a 'hardening-off' firing before glazing. The slip-and-glycerine mixture has the advantage that it can be used on a biscuit pot and then glazed over successfully.

Painting pigments directly on to a pot's surface is ideal for exploiting the qualities of the brushmarks, and you will find that different brushes give marks with different qualities. By experimenting with other methods of applying the colour you can discover many effects. Colour can be applied using fingers, potato-printing, flicking, cloth and scrunched-up paper. Many of the techniques used by interior decorators work well on pottery, and you can use marbling, rag-rolling and dragging to great effect.

31 Mary Rose Young's vibrant and colourful designs are produced by painting underglazes on to 'green' pots and firing with a clear glaze (see 'Underglaze painting' overleaf)

UNDERGLAZE PAINTING

This simple technique involves the use of metal oxides or commercial underglaze colours to paint a design on a clay surface, after which it is covered with a clear glaze and fired. The colours are painted in appropriate strengths and combinations to produce results which will be determined by the chemistry of the clay, colours and glaze.

You can develop your own combinations of materials by mixing them following the guidelines on pages 91–2.

Joe Crouch's pots (figs. 32 and 33) evoke a Mediterranean feeling, with bright, dense colours and unselfconscious brushmarks used to dramatic effect. She has her own shapes made up and delivered in biscuit form, and also makes larger pots by press-moulding and handbuilding.

Trial and error have produced a water-based glycerine-and-slip medium which enables her to apply the colour thickly, without risk of the glaze crawling (rolling into beads and leaving bald patches). She glazes the pots without a hardening-on firing, preferring to use a quick 'in-and-out' dipping technique rather than spraying. The handbuilt pots, which are painted raw, need to be biscuit-fired before glazing.

32 (Right) Joe Crouch builds up her bold designs by painting underglaze slips in layers

33 (Far right) Her 'Mexico' pattern

In contrast, Belen Gomez's pots (figs. 34 and 35) have a light, fairytale quality, with their figurative paintings of maidens in meadows and delicate sailors. Belen draws the images on to the biscuit-fired pots with a pencil, and colours the images using the same underglaze pigment, but in washes and layers to give a watercolour quality. She prefers to mix the colours in water without any medium. The painting is finished with a black outline, and the glaze is sprayed on.

Pigments such as cobalt, copper, iron, manganese and chrome oxides have been used for hundreds of years to produce beautiful, subtle colours and tones. Many contemporary earthenware potters use them to produce lovely painted pots, including David Garland (fig. 36).

As underglaze colours are fritted, their colours are usually similar to those obtained when they are fired with a glaze. (Exceptions to this are dark blues, which are often a purple colour before firing.) Oxides, however, only reveal their true colours when fired with a glaze. An experienced potter will know how thickly to apply an oxide, though a kiln opening will always be a revelation. In contrast, the underglaze painter knows exactly what will happen, as the colours are constant. This can be an advantage!

The recipe section on pages 91–3 explains how to mix oxides to achieve the desired strengths of colour.

34 Belen Gomez painting pots

35 Plates painted by Belen Gomez.
Earthenware with a clear glaze

36 A jug by David Garland. Thrown red
earthenware, coated with white slip and
painted with cobalt, 1991

CHAPTER FOUR

DECORATING WITH SLIPS

Slip decoration, the most ancient of all the painting techniques, has existed ever since the first pots were painted. At its most simple, it can be described as the decoration of one clay using another clay of a different colour.

Slips can be coloured by adding pigments and oxides to the liquid clay. They can be used with a glaze, or for *terra sigillata* and burnished ware.

Slips are often made up of more than just a single clay ingredient: other materials usually need to be added to achieve the desired properties. The ideal slip should 'fit' the clay body and result in the desired surface and colour. 'Fit' means that the slip has a compatible shrinkage with the main body of the pot, and has the correct amount of vitrification at the required firing temperature. As different clays shrink by different amounts, it is often necessary to mix two or more clays together, along with a flux or refractory agent and colouring materials. A bad fit may result in the slip layer flaking off the surface of the pot, a disaster which

can happen long after the pot has been finished. The thickness of the slip has a bearing on this problem (known as 'shelling' or 'flaking') and it is worth avoiding thick patches of slip on rims. Apart from spoiling the pot this can be dangerous, as slivers of slip will often be covered with glaze.

PAINTING WITH SLIPS

A finely sieved slip will be smooth, with an even colour, though interesting results can be otained from slips which have other materials added after sieving (or by sieving through a coarse screen). This is one way to achieve speckles and textures.

Sophie MacCarthy is a major exponent of the art of slip decoration, and her unique approach utilizes techniques of latex resist and paper cut-outs. Unlike most potters who decorate with slips on leatherhard pots, Sophie paints on to bone-dry 'green' (unfired) white earthenware. The sequence of photographs (right and overleaf) shows

Sophie painting one of her fish-and-leaves dishes.

37 and 38   Fish designs by Sophie MacCarthy. (Right, above and below) After the outline of a fish has been drawn on to the pot with a soft pencil, a large, soft brush is loaded with yellow slip which is sloshed over the outline. This is repeated with a pink slip. Unlike slips for trailing or coating leatherhard clay, the slips are very runny because the dry clay surface is absorbent

39   (Far right, above) Once the slip has dried, the outline of the fish is filled in with latex resist. This white, rubbery liquid forms a clear skin, and can be peeled off later without taking off any of the slip layer underneath it

40   (Far right, below) Further layers of coloured slips are built up, pausing for each to dry between coats. Sophie normally paints several pots at once to save time

41 (Above left) Paper leaf shapes are dampened before arranging them on the surface of the pot and painting over them with black slip. Real leaves cannot be used as they tend to disintegrate on contact with the liquid slip

42 and 43 (Left and above) The leaf shapes and then the latex are peeled off to reveal the finished pattern. Details are drawn with a sharp tool and red spots are painted around the leaves. The dish is then biscuit-fired and refired with a clear glaze

44 (Right) A platter by Sophie MacCarthy, with her fish-and-leaves decoration

PAINTING ON A SLIPPED SURFACE

Many potters prefer to coat their leatherhard pots with a layer of slip before painting, to improve or alter the surface. If the pot is made from a gritty clay, for instance, the potter may want to provide a smooth surface by filling in the pit holes with the same clay, sieved to remove the grog. Slips of different clays can also be used.

Dark clays can be covered with white slips to lighten the final colours, or so that lines can be scratched through the slip layer to reveal the darker clay underneath. This is the way I work, and the drawn line is a very important element in my designs. I use a terracotta and white-clay mixture for the pot and a white-clay mixture for the slip. Recipes for these can be found on pages 91 and 92.

Slip can be painted or poured on to the leatherhard pot, or the pot can be dipped in the slip. Trial and error will show the correct thickness, but it is important to remember that very thick slip contains a lot of water, which will be absorbed by the body of the pot, softening it and causing it to collapse. It is better to be patient and paint several layers of a thinner slip, allowing each layer to become leatherhard between coats.

45 *Slipped and painted jug by Mike Levy*

As a guide I find that slip for pouring and dipping should be the consistency of single cream, while slip for painting can be much thicker. I usually have a bucket of each in the workshop, as most of my pots need a combination of techniques.

46   Thrown and turned bowls can be slipped on a rotating wheel with a mop brush. The bowl is placed upside-down on a round batt and is given two or three coats with 'double-cream-thickness' slip, waiting between coats for it to dry (15 minutes; longer in damp weather)

The bowl is then turned over by placing another batt on the foot-ring and quickly flipping it over. Excess slip is removed from the rim with a kidney. The inside and rim are slipped following the same method. When the surface of the slipped pot turns from a creamy-grey to a chalky-white it is ready to be painted

While designing the shape and construction, you should be aware of the processes which the pot is to undergo before it is finished. These can include everything from ease of painting to making sure that an economical number of bowls can fit on to a kiln shelf. With a run of cereal bowls, for example, if you make them half an inch smaller in diameter you may get eleven on a shelf instead of seven, thus decreasing your costs.

Think too about the way you will support the pot while slipping, painting or glazing it. I always give my bowls a flared and reasonably strong turned foot, so that they can be easily and safely held. If the bowl is being pushed down into a bucket of slip I want to be sure that the foot isn't going to give way! This foot is also useful when painting and glazing.

47 (Far left) *Slip can be poured in and out of leatherhard jugs and vases without risk of collapse if the pot is turned* after *pouring. Pouring slip is much quicker than painting it on the insides of jugs and vases*

Pour in the slip until the pot is about half-full, and quickly pour it out while rotating the pot to give even coverage over the inside. A final shake gets rid of any last droplets. The rim is cleaned up with a damp sponge

48 (Left) *After turning, the outside of the pot is painted with two or three coats of thicker slip (typical consistency is that of double cream)*

If the pot is being slipped inside and out it will need to be even in section and reinforced at points of stress. This can minimize most risks. I have recently had to force myself to throw the pots more thickly to reduce the number of collapses.

When applying slip, I normally use a combination of brushing and dipping. I find pouring too uncontrollable and stressful, although it is useful on larger-scale pots. I would rather spend more time being relaxed than a short time in a bad temper!

Mugs, jugs and teapots are assembled after slipping, the joins being touched up when firm with slip on a brush. The various handles, spouts and knobs are made from a white clay with a similar shrinkage to the red body of the pot. This technique has resulted from years of watching joins crack and pots sag and distort when pulled out of shape by their handles after slipping.

In order to make lightweight jugs and vases that can have slip poured inside them without collapsing, I pour the slip in and out before turning (painting the slip inside a jug is very tedious!) This does not work for bowls, due to the architecture of their shape. When slipped, a pot absorbs some of the moisture and expands, but a bowl's rim will expand more than the base, causing the rim to split. A jug's rim is farther away from the unturned base, and the round belly can absorb this difference in expansion. After turning, the outside is brushed with several coats of slip (fig. 48) and the white-clay handle is stuck on

(fig. 49, overleaf). It is possible to use a red-clay handle, but if you want it coated in slip you will find it difficult to do neatly. The only drawback of a white-clay handle is that it cannot be incised to match the rest of the pot.

When the pot has been coated with enough layers (two or three are usually enough to give an opaque layer, depending on the thickness of the slip) it should be left to firm up until it is ready to paint. As the slip layer dries, it turns from a grey-white, which is cold and damp to the touch, to a chalky white with a surface which feels dry and slightly rough.

The best results are obtained when the pot is dry to the touch but still has some moisture in it. This can be tested with a sharp tool or needle, which should cut through the slip easily with a small amount of resistance. If the tool digs into the surface, the pot is too soft. The 'shards' which come off the edges of the line should break away cleanly. If the pot is too dry, the carving will be difficult and will result in a lot of dust. Not only does this give a less confident line, but the dust produced is dangerous and should not be inhaled. Achieving just the right consistency for sgraffito decoration will involve trial and error.

Slipped, leatherhard pots can be kept wrapped in several layers of plastic for weeks without deteriorating. They should be kept away from any direct heat as it will tend to drive out the moisture, which will settle on the plastic covering and result in wet patches

49 Handles, spouts, knobs, etc. are added to the leatherhard slipped body. These are made of a compatible white clay which has the same rate of shrinkage as the red clay. Painting slip on to red handles and spouts is difficult to do neatly, and is more time-consuming.

on the pots. This will happen to some extent anyway, but it need not be a problem in small amounts. Uncovering the pots and leaving them to air for a few minutes soon removes any damp patches.

DRAWING THE DESIGN

I use a very soft graphite pencil to draw the design on the surface of the pot. It is also possible to use ink or watercolour with a brush. Two rules apply here: the material used must burn away in the firing, and the method of application should not mark the surface of the pot. When the pot is at the right consistency, the pencil will make a mark similar to that on cartridge paper.

It is not important for the drawn design to be neat. Some of my larger 'one-off' pieces are covered with scribbles before painting, and only I can decipher the design. All traces of these marks disappear in the biscuit firing, and the pot can look surprisingly clean.

It is important to be satisfied with the design before painting starts, because it is difficult to alter a mistake, especially after the sgraffito lines have been carved. Mistakes can be rectified to some extent by removing the colour with a metal kidney, and then painting white slip over the area. When this slip has firmed up, take the surface back with a kidney and repeat. This fills up the sgraffito lines and rebuilds a flat surface, although small cracks may still appear in the fired pot where the original lines were.

PAINTING THE DESIGN

When you are ready to start painting, you should select your brushes. From a collection of twenty or thirty, there are only three or four that I use on a regular basis. The most useful are square-ended, wide brushes which lay the colour on in even, broad strokes. Fat, pointed brushes are good for figures as they can follow the curves, and a smaller brush is necessary for details. I can probably make do with about five brushes altogether, although it is a real luxury to have two or three of each to save washing them all the time. This also avoids wasting expensive colours.

PREPARATION OF COLOURS

I use a specific range of underglaze colours, mixed in a medium which I have developed over the years to suit my methods best. Although traditional coloured slips are made by mixing an oxide or pigment with white clay slip, I needed a mixture that was more like a paint: strong in colour, which could be applied thickly. After various trials with materials such as egg yolk, linseed oil and honey (all traditional painting media), I found that a 50/50 mixture of glycerine and white slip had the properties I needed.

A small puddle of the glycerine/slip mixture (which should be the consistency of double cream) is put on a plate, and the powdered underglaze colour or oxide is added and mixed in with a spatula until a thick paste is achieved. This can then be diluted by dipping the paintbrush in water and mixing on the plate.

I tend to mix up all my colours at the beginning of a painting session and arrange them around the table in order. Three jars of water save time: one for the yellow/red colours, one for the blue/greens and one for black. This reduces the number of times the water needs changing.

APPLYING COLOURS IN LAYERS

I very rarely leave a coat of only one colour, as applying colours in layers modifies the shades and brings out depths and variations. One colour tends to look flat or thin. I will often paint three blues together in layers, or paint red on top of orange and yellow.

The sequence of photographs on pages 54–60 shows how I paint a large jug with my fish pattern. All the colours used are from the Potterycrafts underglaze range, mixed with the slip/glycerine medium.

The order of painting is determined by the way the colours are used together. Yellow is used first because it is overpainted with both orange and green. Orange comes next, followed by green, pink, red, light and dark blues, and finally black. Other colours are used where necessary.

When painting the yellow first, I fill in areas of the design so that the coloured patches are evenly dispersed around the pot. This is repeated with the other colours to give an even pattern. The rim is painted after the sgraffito, as holding the pot down on the banding wheel causes the colour to smudge, with dirty fingers leaving fingerprints.

50 (Left) The design is drawn on with a very soft graphite pencil, or painted on with ink. Decisions can be made at this stage, as the design can be altered and scribbled over – the pencil marks will disappear in the firing

51 (Right) The underglaze colours are mixed to a thick paste with a 50/50 medium of glycerine and white slip. This can be diluted with water on a brush

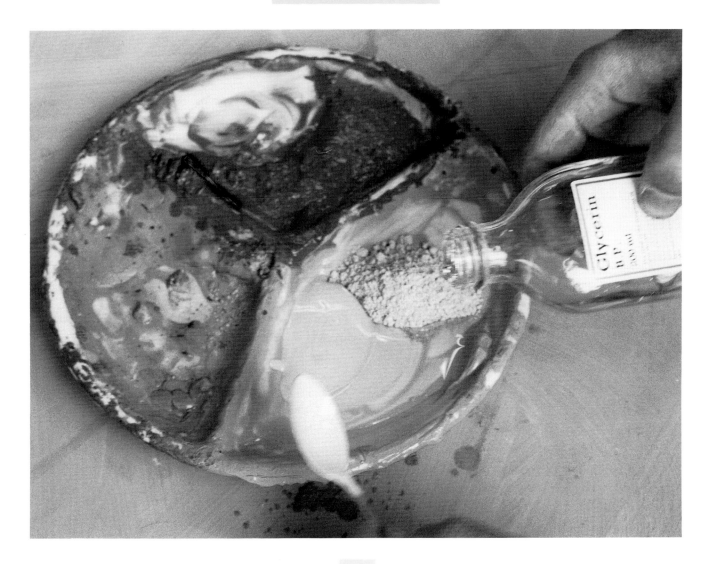

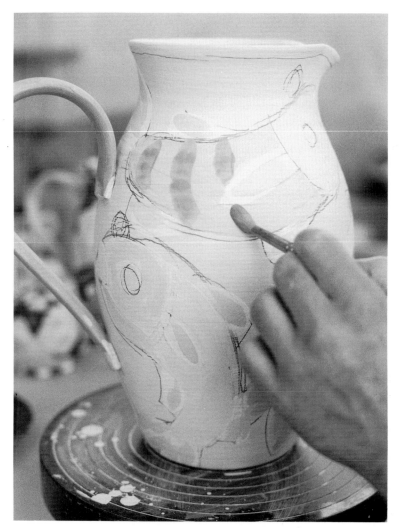

52 *(Far left) The underglaze slips are painted on. I have a particular sequence of yellow, pink, orange, green, blue, red, black, so that I can build up the layers in an efficient order*

53 *(Left) This particular pattern uses wax-resist techniques in the background. The liquid wax is painted over the bright blue and left to dry for about ten minutes*

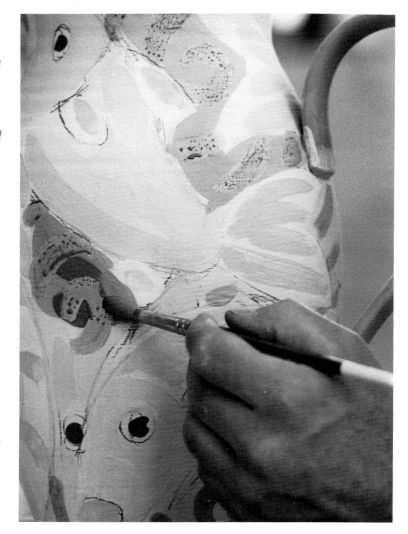

54 *(Right) The dark-blue slip is then painted over the wax, which resists it, leaving isolated droplets. During the glaze-firing the cobalt in the dark blue slip fluxes the glaze and makes it slightly 'runnier' than the glaze over the other colours. This gives a watery feel to the finished pot*

55 (Far left) Using a round-ended, pointed tool, the sgraffito lines are carved. The top rim of the pot is left unpainted at this stage because the pot must be held firmly in place while the lines are carved. It is important to wear a dust mask during this process, as the carving creates a surprisingly large amount of clay dust containing toxic metal oxides. These have a cumulative effect if breathed regularly, and can lead to respiratory and mental problems. Careful regulation of carving pressure can give white sgraffito lines through black slip – note the highlights on the fishes' eyes

56 (Left) The base of the pot is finished by turning it upside-down on the banding wheel – rest it on a folded piece of newspaper as the slipped rim is delicate and can easily chip. The foot rim has the slip removed with a metal kidney

57 (Right) The rim and handle are painted after *the carving has been finished –* otherwise the colour can easily be rubbed off

58 (Far left) Still wearing a dust mask, gently brush the painted pot with a soft Chinese brush to remove excess residue. It is not necessary to be too vigorous, as the colour can be brushed off

59 (Left) After biscuit-firing, the edges of the sgraffito lines are often still sharp. These can be removed by going over the surface of the pot with a grinding-stone from an electric drill. This is easier to manipulate than a traditional grinding-stone and fits the curves inside a bowl better. The dust created by grinding is removed with a stiff 2.5cm (1in) decorator's brush. The pot is then ready to be glazed

60 (Right) Mike Levy in his studio with biscuit-fired pots waiting to be glazed

OTHER SLIP TECHNIQUES

Chinese calligraphy brushes, or those with 'mop' heads, are particularly good for slip as they can hold a lot of liquid in one brushload. To ensure good coverage the slip should be applied fairly thickly, although thin layers can be used to good effect. The best results are obtained by working quickly, as slips tend to show up fussy brushwork. Mistakes can usually be removed by scraping the surface, although this can be difficult if several different layers are involved. It is important not to be too precious about the pot you are working on – too much caution will not only result in mistakes, but will usually produce stiff and lifeless designs.

Shops which sell decorating materials are good sources for painting tools. Sheepskin and textured paint rollers, paint pads, marbling brushes and stipple brushes can all give visually exciting effects. Sponges (natural or synthetic) and textured or scrunched-up cloths can also be used. Interior decorating books are a good source of creative techniques.

SPOTTING

Patterns and designs can be built up by spotting on the slip with the end of a piece of dowel or the edge of a piece of wood. A version of potato cuts also works well, though the potato has to be fairly dry to accept thick slips. Fingers can also be very useful decorating tools, and a lot can be said for smearing on the slip and drawing into it without any help from brushes or bits of wood.

SLIP-TRAILING

Slip-trailing is one of the traditional methods of decorating with slip, and is done simply by applying the mixture through a nozzle, either at the end of a rubber bulb, plastic glue bottle or small washing-up-liquid bottle. This enables the flow of slip to be controlled, producing lines and spots. The technique is similar to the use of an icing-bag in cake decorating, although the slip is runnier than icing.

Slip-trailing takes time and practice to learn, though it is worth the effort as it can produce some fine results. As a method of decorating pots it has been used by potters since Roman times, and there is a fine ongoing tradition of commemorative plates, with lettering applied by slip-trailing. The technique is explained in detail by Anthony Phillips in his book *Slips and Slipware*, also in this series.

BURNISHING

Slips can be used without a glaze, although if left untreated the surface will be matt and easily dirtied, and colours will also be dull. South American pre-Colombian potters treated the surfaces of their pots by burnishing, to seal the surface and produce a beautiful sheen.

The Romans used a similar technique to produce *terra sigillata*. This technique works best with very fine clays and slips that have been sieved through screens of 120s–200s mesh, although almost any smooth clay can be burnished. This effect is destroyed by firing over about 1000°C (1832°F), so be aware that burnished pots are fairly fragile.

Once the pot is made and painted, it can be burnished in the leatherhard state by rubbing the surface all over with a smooth pebble or the back of a spoon. This compresses the fine clay particles on the surface, and the longer the pot is burnished the smoother it will become.

61 (Opposite) Two sun-face vases by Mike Levy. Thrown and slipped earthenware, 12 and 10 inches high, 1990

62   (Left) A handbuilt jar by Kate Byrne, painted with engobes

63   (Above) A handbuilt, painted and burnished pot by Fiona Salazar, 1991

CHAPTER FIVE

GLAZES AND THEIR APPLICATION

Unpacking the kiln after firing pots painted with coloured glazes is probably the most exciting moment in a potter's life. The rows of jars full of muddy grey and brown liquids have little relation to the bright shiny glaze colours which finally emerge. Due to the fact that it is often difficult to tell the difference between two glazes in their unfired state, the potter needs to build up experience when decorating a pot.

64 (Right) A group of pots by Robyn Wilkinson. Flat, shiny colours are obtained from ready-mixed American low-temperature glazes

65 (Far right) This handbuilt vase by Martin Hearne was painted with coloured slips. The line was trailed with a copper-rich engobe, and coloured and clear glazes cover the surface. 1990

A great deal of trial and error can be involved, and each piece is an experiment. Potter Kate Malone, for instance, can fire a pot up to a dozen times, dripping and painting on more layers each time, or grinding patches of glaze off, until she achieves just the effect that she wants (see page 14).

ENGOBES

Engobes (or slip-glazes) are at the dividing point between a slip and a glaze. They can be made to fit leatherhard or biscuited clay and typically have a matt or silky-smooth surface. They can be used in combination with slips and glazes, and have the advantage of great versatility.

Coloured glazes and engobes can be produced from most recipes for clear, white or matt glazes or engobes by the addition of different colouring materials. Figs. 66–8 show Kate Byrne decorating a large, handbuilt, white earthenware pot with a combination of slips, engobes and glazes.

66 Engobe painting by Kate Byrne. (Above right) Washes of thin slips are painted over the surface of the bone-dry pot

67 (Right) Thicker engobes are applied to particular areas with a fairly dry brush to build up a textured surface

68 (Above) A design is carved through the layers to reveal the white clay. Engobes can be carved as if they were slips, while having similar fired qualities to glaze. All dust should be cleaned up with a wet sponge immediately. After biscuit-firing, Kate applies coloured glazes and engobes to the surface and fires the pot a second time

69 (Right) Large dish by Mike Levy. Thrown and slipped earthenware, 16 inches in diameter, 1991

70 *(Opposite) Handbuilt vase and jug by Liz Beckenham. Red earthenware with burnished slip decoration, 1991*

71 *(Left) A seventeenth-century English jug with slip-trailed and spotted bird decoration (British Museum)*

TIN GLAZING

Tin glazing was developed by Islamic potters to imitate the whiteness of porcelain. The technique came to Italy from Spain via Majorca, where it became known as majolica.

When a clear glaze has tin oxide added it becomes an opaque white. Oxides and glaze stains can be added to small amounts of this glaze, and painted on to the unfired glaze surface. When the pot is fired, the layers of glaze melt together to produce beautiful soft effects. Similar effects can be obtained by covering a white earthenware pot with a clear glaze and painting on the surface with underglazes and oxides mixed with glaze.

MAJOLICA

Working with the traditional Italian technique of majolica (also known as in-glaze or tin glaze), Daphne Carnegy produces fine tableware covered with paintings of fruit and flowers in broad, lively brushstrokes (see pages 18 and 71–5).

72   An Italian Renaissance majolica tile from the seventeenth century, featuring a Madonna-and-Child scene (British Museum)

The biscuited red-clay pot is coated with a glaze that has a high proportion of tin oxide, which makes it an opaque white with a satin-smooth surface. When the glaze is dry, the surface can be painted. On firing, the pigments sink into the glaze surface and 'stain' it. This can produce beautiful soft colours as well as lovely mottled areas. Figs. 73–7 show Daphne decorating a pot and one of her mugs.

The colours used should be mixed with a small amount of glaze or flux, so that the glaze is not dry from the addition of a refractory material. Some colouring oxides (such as cobalt) work as a flux, and these have to be applied thinly or modified. Interesting results can be obtained from deliberately letting the colours run. This technique can also be used with a clear glaze over white clay.

73 After waxing the areas of the pot which are to be left unglazed (such as the foot-ring), the pot is glazed and left to dry. The design is drawn on with a soft pencil and the coloured glaze or pigment is painted in layers

74 and 75 *The colours are applied one-by-one to build up the design*

*76 and 77   Some of Daphne Carnegy's
patterns have a dark background with a
white outline. This is achieved by painting
hot wax around the design and the rim, and
then filling in the background with a flat
brush
   During the glaze firing the colours sink into
the glaze surface to produce beautiful colours
and textures*

ENAMELS

Enamels are glazes with a low firing temperature, and are used to decorate an already-glazed surface. They were traditionally formulated with lead compounds to lower the firing temperature. They are now made according to strict health-and-safety regulations, though it is still imperative to follow the manufacturer's instructions and to avoid breathing or ingesting any dust or powder. This applies as a general rule in the pottery studio: always take care with all ceramic materials and never eat or drink in the workshop.

Industrially produced tableware is often decorated with enamel transfers. These are designs printed with enamel inks on large sheets of waxed paper. The individual designs are then over-printed with a gel which enables them to be floated off the sheet in water. These are then stuck to the shiny surface of a glazed mug or plate, and fired.

The same materials can also be used for painting by hand on white china as well as factory- or hand-produced earthenware or stoneware.

78   A glazed earthenware plate painted with enamels, by Julie Arkell, 1990

Enamels are colouring pigments which are mixed with a flux so that they mature at relatively low temperatures (usually around 750–850°C [1382–1562°F]). This means that pigments which burn out at higher temperatures can be used to produce a very wide palette of colours.

The surface of the pot should be free from grease, as this can inhibit the adhesion of the colours (many china painters wear cotton gloves for this reason). You should also try to keep the work area as dust-free as possible, as dust can easily mark the pot's surface.

You will find a medium which suits you by trying out different materials. Traditionally, the colours are ground in fat-oil of turpentine and diluted with pure turpentine. Sugar solutions, honey, golden syrup and glycerine

79 The powdered-enamel colours are mixed using a syrup medium. A spatula is used to grind the powder and syrup into a smooth paste. Water is added on the brush to dilute the paste to the desired consistency. It should be possible to paint on the glazed surface without raised brushmarks or runs and dribbles.

also work well, and have the advantage of being water-based and not giving off unpleasant fumes. It is most important to choose a medium which allows the colour to cover the surface smoothly, and which will not be easily brushed off when packing the kiln. Unfired enamels are very fragile, and care must be taken not to scratch them as every detail, including scratches, will remain after firing.

Enamels should be fired slowly to enable the medium to burn off gently, and the kiln and kiln room should be well ventilated. If an oil-based medium is used, the kiln will give off foul-smelling smoke. It is not advisable to be in the same room as a kiln which is firing enamel glazes. Typical firing temperatures are between 700–800°C (1292–1472°F).

80 *Josie Firmin draws the design in black directly on to the glazed surface with a nib pen. The nib is loaded with enamel using a brush*

81 The outlines are filled in with colours. Enamel colours can be painted on top of each other, and their transparent nature can lead to some lovely effects

82 (Overleaf) The firing gives the colours a smooth, glossy, permanent surface. This group of bone china, enamel-painted pots is from the Cosmo Place Workshop, London

APPLYING GLAZES

Most studio potters biscuit-fire their pots before applying the glaze, as this has many advantages. It is possible to glaze raw pots – in fact all pottery was raw-glazed before the advent of the studio potter earlier this century. Techniques of raw glazing are very tricky: the pots have to be bone-dry, and the dipping and pouring must be quick and efficient. In addition, there is only one attempt at glazing a pot, whereas with biscuit-fired pots the glaze can be washed off and re-applied if necessary.

There are four basic methods of applying a glaze to a biscuited pot: dipping, pouring, painting and spraying.

DIPPING

This is my chosen method, and if done properly it can be a calm experience. If, however, you have not tidied the workbench and moved all clutter away from the floor you will have an annoying and frustrating time.

In order to glaze pots by dipping you need a large, clean bench, an assortment of buckets and bowls, an 80s-mesh sieve, two batons, a small scrubbing brush, a paintbrush and a sponge. Waxing any areas to be left unglazed (i.e., feet) beforehand is a good idea, although the glaze can easily be removed with a sponge after dipping.

It is usually necessary to sieve the glaze each time you need to glaze a batch of pots, as dry patches of glaze on the sides of the bucket can fall in and form lumps. Sponging down the inside and outside of the bucket after glazing can prevent this. Rest the sieve on the two batons placed across the top of a bucket, and pour the glaze through slowly while moving a small scrubbing brush in circles on the mesh.

Experience will determine the thickness of the glaze for your particular needs, but, as a guide, a biscuited pot fired to 1000°C (1832°F) will need glaze the consistency of single cream. My pots are biscuited to 1140°C (2084°F), and my glaze is almost as thick as custard.

If you are using a clear glaze over painted decoration, try and apply the glaze thinly for best results, although not so thinly that the surface is rough. Coloured and tin glazes can be thicker.

Choose a suitable bowl or bucket, deep enough to accommodate the pot and one or two hands. Large bowls can be glazed in a larger, shallow dish if you don't have enough glaze to completely immerse the bowl. By holding the bowl with fingers spread apart on either side of the rim, it can be rotated through the glaze and lifted clear, leaving the surplus glaze to pour back into the bucket.

With your sleeves rolled up, and your wrists and elbows always above the bowl or bucket, a smaller pot can be dipped into the glaze by holding it in one hand, with your forefinger on the foot and your thumb on the rim. Swirl it around and remove it with a sweep. Hold the pot up with your hand beneath it, so that the surplus glaze runs down your hand and drips off your wrist or elbow back into the bucket.

Hold the pot until the shine has gone from the surface of the glaze. It can now be placed on the bench and the next pot can be glazed. When all the pots have been glazed, touch up the fingermarks with a paintbrush dipped in the glaze.

The pots should be left to dry, and any unwanted ridges on the glaze surface can then be fettled using a metal kidney. (Always wear a mask when fettling to avoid breathing the dust.) Sponge any glaze off the foot-ring before firing.

POURING

This is a useful technique when the pot to be glazed is large or a difficult shape to manipulate. It does not require a great amount of glaze or large buckets.

You will need a good-sized, shallow bowl or bucket, a jug large enough to hold one to two litres of glaze (I use a selection of white enamel jugs and bowls found on market stalls and at junk yards over the years) and two batons. The jug should not be so large that it is difficult to lift when full of glaze, as pouring should be done evenly. A heavy banding wheel is optional.

The batons are placed over the empty bucket and the biscuited pot is supported upside-down on them. The glaze is in the jug with another bucket of glaze handy. The bucket should stand on a stool so that it is possible to walk round it while the glaze is poured over the pot. Alternatively, stand the bucket on the large banding wheel so that it can be rotated while the glaze is poured.

Pour the glaze over the pot while moving round the stool, or rotate the wheel while pouring. Any surplus glaze will end up in the bucket. Plates and platters can be supported on a hand which tilts and rotates as the glaze is poured.

Once the glaze on the outside of the pot has dried, the glaze can be poured inside, swirled around and poured out. Excess patches of glaze can be fettled off as before.

PAINTING
This is possible with some glazes, and can be used to great effect. If a flat colour is desired, it is worth noting that brushed glazes can have patchy surfaces. 'Mop-head' brushes can hold a lot of glaze in one go and are useful for applying large strokes. Glaze can be dabbed on to the pot in patches for decorative effect (see Kate Malone's technique on page 14). Robyn Wilkinson uses commercial glazes designed for painting on her handbuilt pots (see page 65).

Painting is often used in conjunction with other methods and for touching up surfaces.

SPRAYING
This is only possible in a well-equipped studio. It should be done in a spray booth fitted with suitable extractor equipment, and, although it can be extremely accurate, it is wasteful as some of the excess glaze is extracted to the atmosphere (glaze deposited on the inside of the spray booth can be washed off and reclaimed). Spraying puts fine particles of glaze into the air and can therefore be hazardous to health, so a face mask should always be used. It is advisable to have proper instruction in the use of compressors and spray guns before using this method.

As it is not possible to spray into enclosed areas, these must be glazed by pouring beforehand. The pot is then placed on a banding wheel within the spray booth, and, as the pot rotates, the glaze is sprayed in a fine mist of particles suspended in water, through a spray gun attached to a compressor.

Spraying is good for large and awkwardly shaped pots, giving even results. Glazes can be blended and graded into each other.

CHAPTER SIX

DECORATED TILES

Tiles are relatively quick and simple to make. Decorated tiles may consist of individual, 'one-off' paintings, or can be used in greater quantities to cover a large area. There is a long historical tradition of painted tiles from China, the Middle East, southern Europe and Holland, and inspiration can be gleaned from their many different shapes, colours and designs.

83 A selection of tin-glazed tiles by Carlo Briscoe and Eddie Dunn captures the spirit of Delft tiles. They are made by rolling out the white earthenware clay into slabs and cutting them into squares using a template. When dry, the tiles are biscuit-fired and then glazed. The in-glaze images are painted (see pages 70–5) and the tiles are fired to 1060°C (1940°F)

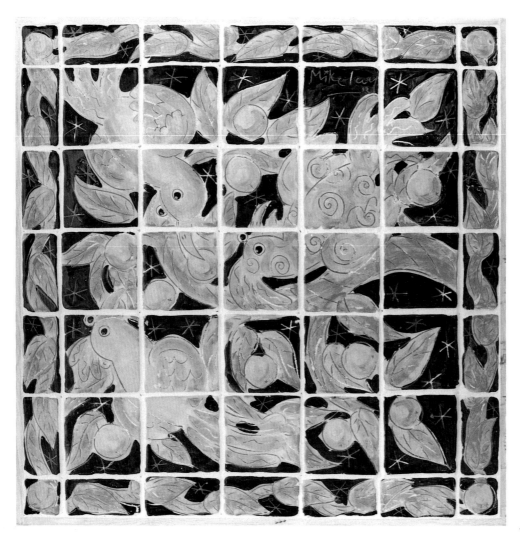

84 *A tile panel by Mike Levy. The making process is explained on the following pages. After glaze-firing the tiles were mounted on plywood and grouted*

Tiles were the most widespread product of the Dutch tin-glaze centres, and were used to adorn the walls of kitchens and dairies, as well as for skirting-boards and decorative pictures. Islamic tiles are particularly renowned for their interlocking shapes, complicated repeat designs and intricate lettering. These are used extensively to decorate mosques and prayer niches. Spanish, Italian and Mexican hand-made tiles are popular today for use in kitchens and bathrooms. Samples of these can be seen in specialist tile shops, and form another source of inspiration.

All the decorating techniques described earlier in the book are suitable for use with tiles. Factory-made biscuited tiles are widely available from materials suppliers (see page 95), and may be painted with underglazes or coloured glazes to produce beautiful results. The alternative is of course to make your own tiles for decorating.

MAKING TECHNIQUES

Tiles can be made by simply rolling out a slab of clay, cutting it into squares and leaving them to dry. They can also be press-moulded and extruded. Although the tiles shown in the following sequence of photographs are square in shape, press-moulding can be used to produce more complicated shapes. You may find that flat clay pieces have a tendency to warp, but using the following techniques will help to minimize this problem.

1 Use a grogged clay. This should also make the soft tiles easier to handle.

2 Prepare the clay with the minimum of kneading. Clay is made up of smooth, plate-like particles which 'line up' in the same direction when the clay is kneaded. This gives the clay a tendency to curve on drying. Clay which has not been kneaded consists of random particles and is less likely to warp.

3 Cut a block of clay into slabs with a wire, rather than 'thumping' it down and rolling it with a rolling pin, as rolling has the same effect as kneading.

4 If the tiles are press-moulded, leave them in the mould until they can be handled without bending.

5 Dry the tiles on an absorbent surface or a baking rack. This will allow the tiles to dry evenly, lessening the risk of warping.

6 Leave the tiles to dry out fully between wooden boards, to restrict movement. Some manufacturers dry and store tiles in stacks with weights on the top to 'press' them flat.

85 (Far left, top), *86 (Far left, bottom),* *87 (Left, top)* **and** *88 (Left, bottom)   The clay is rolled out and pressed into a plaster mould. The edges are finished with a plastic wallpaper scraper (metal will damage the mould, and plaster impurities in the clay may lead to problems later)*

89   (Above right) After about an hour the tiles will be leatherhard and can be removed from the mould with a soft piece of clay. The edges are finished with a damp sponge

90   (Right) The tile is held by its edges and dipped into a bucket of slip (double-cream thickness)

91 *(Far left, top) After shaking to remove excess slip, the tiles are left to dry on a board*

92 *(Far left, bottom) When leatherhard, the tiles are arranged in the shape of the panel and the design is drawn on with soft pencil*

93 and 94 *(Left, top and bottom) The colours are painted on and allowed to dry (see pages 53–60)*

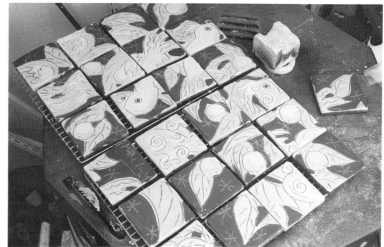

95 *(Above right) The lines are carved through the colours to reveal the red-clay body*

96 *(Right) The tiles are left to dry on baking racks*

97 This panel was made by cutting a leatherhard slab of clay into sections to a design drawn on the surface. Each piece was slipped, painted and carved, and the panel was re-assembled after glazing (Mike Levy)

CHAPTER SEVEN

RECIPES

CLAYS

Earthenware clays range from a deep chocolate-brown to a creamy-white. Although it is possible to dig and prepare your own clay, this is only worth the quite considerable effort if the clay is in your back yard, has particular qualities, or you are doing it for philosophical reasons!

You will almost certainly be able to find a clay from a supplier which will suit your needs, and most potters are lucky enough to be able to order clay by telephone and have it delivered to the workshop. Earthenware clays are relatively cheap to buy in bags, and the price gets cheaper the more you order. The clay can be used straight from the bag, with a small amount of wedging and kneading.

I use a mixture of three clays, which has been developed to give me a red clay with properties compatible with the white slip I use to coat it. This has a rate of shrinkage lower than pure-red earthenware at the temperature at which I fire my pots.

The properties I need from my clay are:

1 Deep-enough colour to show as a deep brown when seen as a carved line (neat red clay was too dark).
2 Pale-enough colour to be easily covered by a thin layer of slip, reducing the danger of shelling on the rims.
3 Good responsiveness for throwing, with the strength to make large shapes.
4 Enough grog to give strength, but not too much: grog can interfere with the sgraffito lines and give a scratchy surface when turning.

I found three clays from Potclays which, when mixed in equal parts, give me exactly the properties that I need. I mix each new mixture 50/50 with reclaimed clay, which is more plastic. These clays are numbers 1135 (red), LT25 (white) and LT25/30 (white with grog). LT25 is a very good clay for throwing and handbuilding.

Although mixing clay by hand is a chore, in practice it needs to be done only rarely. I tend to spend a whole day every six months doing this, and efficient reclaiming of turnings and discarded pots means that I always have some clay drying out on a batt which can be wedged and used.

Clays are also available in powdered form for mixing clays and making slips. If you are mixing clay in this way, remember that it needs to sit for a while to become more workable.

UNDERGLAZES

Oxides and carbonates of earth metals can be used to great effect in underglazes, and can be mixed to produce a wide palette. The percentage amounts given are for addition to glazes; slips and clay bodies will need more. When used for underglaze painting, mix with water, put through a 200s-mesh sieve and dilute to the required strength. CARE MUST BE TAKEN WITH THESE MATERIALS, AS MANY ARE POISONOUS.

CHROMIUM OXIDE

Usually producing an opaque green, chromium oxide will give a grass-green when used with calcium, and a blue-green with cobalt and magnesium. Pink can be obtained in high-alkaline tin glaze. Use 1–3% in glaze.

COBALT OXIDE/CARBONATE

The most powerful of the colouring pigments, cobalt carbonate is less strong and speckles less than the oxide. It produces a deep blue, or a bright blue in an alkaline glaze. Very small amounts should be used (1–2%). Cobalt is a flux and will make glazes runnier. When used with magnesium the colour tends more towards purple.

COPPER OXIDE/CARBONATE

Typically green, copper gives turquoise in an alkaline glaze. The carbonate disperses more easily than the oxide and does not speckle. Use up to 5% in glazes.

Copper has the property of making low-solubility lead glazes more soluble. These glazes should therefore never be used on vessels intended for food use.

IRON OXIDES/CHROMATE

There are many compounds of iron that have different strengths and colours.

1   Iron chromate: grey, brown or black (1–6%).
2   Iron oxide (red): honey to dark brown (2–10%).
3   Iron oxide (black): dark browns; black with cobalt (4–8%).
4   Iron oxide (yellow ochre): yellowish-browns (3–8%).

Other forms are also available, giving slightly different effects.

MANGANESE DIOXIDE/CARBONATE

In lead and low-alkaline glazes, manganese gives pink to brown, while in high-alkaline glaze the colour is nearer purple (0.25–5%). Use with cobalt and iron to produce black.

NICKEL OXIDE

Normally used to modify other colours, nickel will give grey in barium or lead glazes, tan with calcium and bright green with magnesium. With large quantities of zinc it produces lavender-blue.

INDUSTRIALLY PRODUCED UNDERGLAZE COLOURS

Available from pottery suppliers, these colours have improved greatly in recent years, and it is now possible to get good-quality reds and oranges which fire to high temperatures. Each supplier has their own range, and some colours are better than others. These can be mixed to obtain intermediate colours, and can be mixed with tin oxide to produce opaque pastels.

Underglaze colours are produced by refining, firing and grinding oxides to produce inert, stable powders. Their colours are similar to the final fired colour (with the exception of blues, which appear purple in the powdered form).

SLIPS

Slips can be liquid versions of clays, or can be mixed from powdered materials. A basic white slip (used at Harrow College) consists of ball clay SMD (60%) and China clay (40%) and I have yet to find a recipe superior to this for sgraffito.

For a blue slip, add 4% of cobalt carbonate to white slip.

For a black slip, add 4% of cobalt carbonate to red slip.

Orange and cream slips can be made by adding the red and white slips together, while the blue and black slips can also be mixed to produce other colours.

Body stains or underglazes can be added to slips in proportions of up to 15%, though this is an expensive way of colouring and should only be used if it is impossible to obtain the colour by another means.

ENGOBES

Engobes are an intermediate stage between slips and glazes. A basic engobe recipe which can be used as a starting point to develop your own recipes is made up of the following components:

4 parts ball clay
5 parts China clay
1 part tin oxide, zirconium silicate (zircon) or disperzon
2 parts borax frit

This engobe can be applied to raw and biscuit surfaces, and will fire to between 1120 and 1160°C (2048 and 2120°F). By adjusting the amounts of clay and frit you can alter the shine of the fired surface.

TERRA SIGILLATA

Terra sigillata is the fine slip used by the Ancient Greeks for their black-on-red painting, and which Fiona Salazar uses for burnishing (see page 64). It is made by mixing red clay (or white ball clay for white slip) with water to make a thin slip. Some deflocculant may be added to keep the particles in suspension (approximately 0·3% sodium hydroxide to the dry clay weight is recommended by Daniel Rhodes in Clay and Glazes for the Potter).

The slip is mixed and left to settle for a few days, after which the water is poured off and the fine top-third of the slip is taken off for use. The rest of the slip is discarded. Pots painted with terra sigillata can be burnished and fired to around 900–1000°C (1652–1832°F).

GLAZES

Glazes give a pot a protective, sealed surface. They can be glossy, smooth or matt, clear or opaque, and can have a variety of colours. My personal choice of glaze comes ready-mixed in a bag from the suppliers, but you may prefer to mix your own. As I use a clear glaze on all my pots, it is convenient not to have bags of many different materials around the workshop. However, you may wish to develop a glaze that has particular properties, and this is much easier if you know the ingredients.

Glazes can be formulated to produce a wide range of interesting colours and surfaces. If you wish to make glazes from recipes or to develop your own, I would recommend The Potter's Book of Glaze Recipes by Emmanuel Cooper (Batsford, 1989) for a wide range of surface effects.

In her book Mary Wondrausch on Slipware, Mary Wondrausch gives a clear glaze recipe of:

75% lead sesquisilicate
18% China clay
 6% flint

Daphne Carnegy's tin-glaze recipe is as follows:

60% lead bisilicate
 9% standard borax frit
15% Cornish stone
 5% China clay
 7% tin oxide
 7% zirconium silicate
 2% zinc oxide
 2% bentonite

The firing range is between 1060 and 1160°C (1940 and 2120°F). Daphne Carnegy fires her glaze kiln to Orton 01.

This glaze is used to cover a pink earthenware mixture of Potclays Buff and Red S/E clays in a proportion of 4:1. If the pots are to hold liquids, a 1:1 mixture is used for a higher degree of vitrification.

RECOMMENDED COMMERCIAL GLAZES

Mike Levy and Joe Crouch both use Potterycrafts P2038 or Ceramatech CT 2330; Belen Gomez uses Potterycrafts P2019. Ceramatech CT 2330 has good craze resistance.

All these glazes give good colour response, and can be used with oxides and glaze stains. Remember not to use copper as a stain in a lead-based glaze on pots for food use.

FURTHER READING

Anscombe, Isabelle. *Omega and After – Bloomsbury and the Decorative Arts*, Thames & Hudson, 1981

Buckley, Cheryl. *Potters and Paintresses – Women Designers in the Pottery Industry 1870–1955*, The Women's Press, 1990

Charleston, R. J. *World Ceramics*, Hamlyn, 1968

Clark, Kenneth. *The Potter's Manual*, Macdonald, 1983

Cooper, Emmanuel. *A History of World Pottery*, Batsford, 1988

Hamer, Frank. *The Potter's Dictionary of Materials and Techniques*, Pitman, 1975

Hamilton, David. *Manual of Pottery and Ceramics*, Thames & Hudson, 1974

Lane, Peter. *Studio Ceramics*, Collins, 1983

Naylor, Gillian. *Bloomsbury*, Bullfinch, 1990

Perez-Tibi, Dora. *Dufy*, Thames & Hudson, 1989

Rhodes, Daniel. *Clay and Glazes for the Potter*, Pitman House, 1973

Williams, Dyfri. *Greek Vases*, British Museum Publications, 1985

Wilson, Timothy. *Ceramic Art of the Italian Renaissance*, British Museum Publications, 1987

Wondrausch, Mary. *Mary Wondrausch on Slipware*, A. & C. Black, 1986

SUPPLIERS

ENGLAND

Ceramatech Ltd
Unit 16 Frontier Works
33 Queen Street
London NI7 8JA
Tel: 081–885 4492

Potterycrafts Ltd
Campbell Road
Stoke-on-Trent ST4 4ET
Tel: 0782–745000

Potclays Ltd
Brick Kiln Lane
Etruria
Stoke-on-Trent ST4 7BP
Tel: 0782–219816

The Fulham Pottery Ltd
8–10 Ingate Place
Battersea
London SW8 3NS
Tel: 071–720 0050

Reward-Clayglaze Ltd
Kingsyard Pottery
Talbot Road
Rickmansworth
Hertfordshire WD3 1HW
Tel: 0923 770127

SCOTLAND

Techtex Scotland Ltd
Braehead
Gouldry
Newport-on-Tay
Fife DD6 8RQ
Tel: 0826 24259

IRELAND

Scarva Pottery Supplies
10 Drummiller Lane
Scarva
Co. Armagh BT63 6BR
Tel: 0762 831864

USA

Westwood Ceramic Supply Co.
14400 Iomitas Avenue
Dept B067 City of Industry
California 91746

Amaco American Art Clay Co. Inc.
4717 West Sixteenth Street
Indianapolis
Indiana 46222

Randall Pottery Inc.
Box 774
Alfred
New York 14802

Kentucky-Tennessee Clay Co.
Box 449
Mayfield
Kentucky 42066

AUSTRALIA

Diamond Ceramic Supplies Ltd
50–52 Geddes Street
Mulgrave
Melbourne
Victoria 3170

Ceramic Supply Co.
61 Lakemba Street
Belmore
NSW 2192

Walker Ceramics
Boronia Road
Wantirna
Victoria
PO Box 208
Bayswater 3153

Pottery Supplies Pty Ltd
51 Castlemain Street
Milton
Brisbane 4064

INDEX

94,01

DATE DUE			

GAYLORD
M2